smoothies & juices

fruit smoothies • veggie smoothies
dessert smoothies • juices

mc rae
PUBLISHING

This book was conceived, edited and designed by McRae Publishing Ltd London

www.mcraepublishing.co.uk

NOTE TO OUR READERS
Eating eggs or egg whites that are not completely cooked poses the possibility of salmonella food poisoning. The risk is greater for pregnant women, the elderly, the very young, and persons with impaired immune systems. If you are concerned about salmonella, you can use reconstituted powdered egg whites or pasteurized eggs.

Culinary Notebooks series

Project Director Anne McRae
Art Director Marco Nardi

SMOOTHIES & JUICES
Photography Brent Parker Jones
Text Carla Bardi
Editing Foreign Concept
Food Styling Lee Blaylock
Food Styling Assistant Rochelle Seator
Prop Styling Lee Blaylock
Layouts Sara Fellowes

ISBN 978-88-6098-294-0

Printed in China

contents

getting started

There are more than 100 delicious recipes for smoothies and juices in this book. They are all very fast and easy to prepare, making them ideal for quick-fix snacks and busy weekday breakfasts. We have also included a chapter on dessert smoothies to finish up healthy meals. You will need a blender to make the smoothies and a juicer to extract the juices. In these pages we have chosen 25 of the most enticing recipes, just to get you started.

 SIMPLE

CITRUS & PARSLEY juice

BLUEBERRY
smoothies

SPINACH & PEAR
smoothies

BANANA & STRAWBERRY
SMOOTHIES with
chocolate & cream

BERRY BEST juice

BANANA & PEACH
SMOOTHIES with wheat germ

STRAWBERRY & OATMEAL
breakfast smoothies

SUPER HEALTHY

SPICY CARROT, APPLE & CUCUMBER juice

CILANTRO & ALMOND
detox smoothies

SPINACH, SOY & WHEAT
JUICE with ginko

DAIRY-FREE SMOOTHIES

SOY & BERRYFRUIT smoothies

YELLOW & GREEN
layered smoothies

MELON & KIWI
smoothies

CRANBERRY & ORANGE
tofu smoothies

WATERMELON
& CRANBERRY
soy smoothies

CARIBBEAN
smoothies

CARROT & LIME
smoothies

EDITOR'S CHOICE

MANGO & YOGURT smoothies

CHOCOLATE
CAPPUCCINO smoothies

HOMEMADE TOMATO
juice

BEST FRUIT SMOOTHIE

CHERRY & RASPBERRY
smoothies

BEST VEGGIE SMOOTHIE

CARROT, APPLE
& CUCUMBER smoothies

BEST DESSERT SMOOTHIE

BANANA SMOOTHIES
with chocolate & nuts

BEST SMOUSSIE

RASPBERRY & WHITE
CHOCOLATE smoussies

BEST JUICE

AVOCADO JUICE
with wasabi

fruit smoothies

YELLOW & GREEN layered smoothies

1 small fresh pineapple, peeled, tough core removed, and chopped
1 cup (250 ml) crushed ice
4 kiwi fruit

Serves 2 • Preparation 15 minutes • Difficulty 1

1. Place two tall glasses in the freezer to chill.
2. Combine the pineapple and $1/2$ cup (120 ml) of the crushed ice in a blender and blend until smooth. Pour into the glasses and replace in the freezer.
3. Rinse the blender then chop the kiwi fruit with the remaining $1/2$ cup (120 ml) of crushed ice until smooth.
4. Pour the green kiwi mixture carefully in on top of the pineapple mixture to make layered smoothies.

If you liked this recipe, you will love these as well.

COLADA smoothies

MELON & KIWI smoothies

PINEAPPLE & ALMOND smoothies

Fresh in-season cherries are a treat to eat, and they are also a good source of vitamins C and K and dietary fiber. Cherries contain a variety of phytochemicals that are linked to lower rates of cancer and heart disease. They are also believed to improve the immune system.

BANANA & CHERRY SMOOTHIES
with raspberries & cream

1   banana
1   cup (150 g) fresh raspberries + few extra to garnish
1   cup (250 ml) unsweetened cherry juice
1   cup (250 ml) crushed ice
    Whipped cream, to serve (optional)

Serves 2 • Preparation 10 minutes • Difficulty 1

1. Place two serving glasses in the freezer to chill.
2. Combine the banana, raspberries, cherry juice, and ice in a blender and blend until smooth and slushy.
3. Pour into the glasses. Top with the cream, if using, and 1–2 whole raspberries

If you liked this recipe, you will love these as well.

20
CHERRY & RASPBERRY smoothies

72
CHERRY smoothies

98
FENNEL & CHERRY juice

BANANA & LEMON SMOOTHIES with mint

1	banana
	Freshly squeezed juice of 1 lemon
1	cup (250 g) lemon yogurt
½	cup (75 g) seedless green grapes
1-2	tablespoons honey
1	tablespoon fresh mint leaves + extra leaves to garnish
6	ice cubes

Serves 2 • Preparation 10 minutes • Difficulty 1

1. Place two tall glasses in the freezer to chill.

2. Combine the banana, lemon juice, yogurt, grapes, honey, mint leaves, and ice in a blender and blend until smooth.

3. Pour into the glasses, garnish with the mint, and serve.

BANANA & PEACH SMOOTHIES
with wheat germ

1   banana
1   cup (250 ml) low-fat vanilla yogurt
¼   cup (60 ml) freshly squeezed orange juice
¼   cup (30 g) wheat germ + extra to dust
½   cup (120 ml) crushed ice
2   peaches, pitted and sliced

Serves 2 • Preparation 10 minutes • Difficulty 1

1. Place two glasses in the freezer to chill. Reserve 2 slices of peach to garnish.

2. Combine the banana, yogurt, orange juice, wheat germ, ice, and remaining peaches in a blender and blend until smooth.

3. Pour into the glasses and garnish with the slices of peach. Dust with extra wheat germ and serve.

Soy milk, also known as soya milk or soybean milk, is made by soaking dried soybeans and grinding them with water. Soy milk has about the same amount of protein as cow's milk. It is ideal for people with lactose intolerance or milk allergies.

SOY & BERRYFRUIT smoothies

1	cup (150 g) fresh strawberries
2	cups (500 ml) vanilla soy milk
2	cups (300 g) fresh or frozen blueberries

Serves 2 • Preparation 10 minutes • Difficulty 1

1. Place two tall glass in the freezer to chill. Halve or slice one or two of the fresh strawberries and reserve to garnish.
2. Combine the soy milk, blueberries, and remaining strawberries in a blender and blend until smooth.
3. Pour into the glasses, garnish with the reserved strawberries, and serve.

If you liked this recipe, you will love these as well.

BLUEBERRY
smoothies

CHERRY & RASPBERRY
smoothies

BLUEBERRY & ALMOND
smoothies

PEAR & GRAPE smoothies

Serves 2 • Preparation 10 minutes • Difficulty 1

3	large ripe pears, peeled and cored	1	avocado
1	cup (150 g) seedless white grapes + 2-3 extra to garnish	3	tablespoons freshly squeezed lime juice
		1	tablespoon honey

1. Place two glasses in the freezer to chill.

2. Combine the pears, grapes, avocado, lime juice, and honey in a blender and blend until smooth.

3. Pour into the chilled glasses. Thread the extra grapes onto toothpicks and lay them across the glasses to garnish. Serve.

BANANA PASSION smoothies

Serves 2 • Preparation 10 minutes • Difficulty 1

1	cup (250 ml) plain yogurt	2	teaspoons honey
2	small ripe bananas		Banana slices, with skin, to garnish
	Strained pulp of 4 passion fruit		Fresh mint, to garnish

1. Place two wine goblets in the freezer to chill.

2. Combine the yogurt, bananas, passion fruit pulp, and honey in a blender and blend until smooth.

3. Pour into the chilled wine goblets. Garnish with the banana and mint and serve.

COLADA smoothies

Serves 2 • Preparation 10 minutes • Difficulty 1

1	cup (250 ml) pineapple juice	1/4	cup (60 ml) freshly squeezed lime juice
1/2	cup (120 ml) cream of coconut	4	tablespoons crushed ice
1/4	cup (60 ml) heavy (double) cream		Wedges of fresh pineapple, to garnish

1. Place two large wine goblets in the freezer to chill.

2. Combine the pineapple juice, cream of coconut, cream, and lime juice in a blender and blend until smooth.

3. Divide the crushed ice evenly between the chilled wine goblets and pour the smoothie mixture in over the top. Garnish with the pineapple and serve.

BLUEBERRY smoothies

Serves 2 • Preparation 10 minutes • Difficulty 1

3	cups (450 g) fresh blueberries	2	teaspoons honey
1	cup (250 ml) milk	10	ice cubes, crushed
1/2	cup (120 ml) thick, Greek-style yogurt		

1. Place two large glasses in the freezer to chill.

2. Combine the blueberries, milk, yogurt, honey, and ice in a blender and blend until smooth and thick.

3. Pour into the chilled glasses. Serve immediately.

Fresh mangoes are an excellent source of vitamins A and C, beta-carotenes, and potassium. They are believed to help lower blood pressure and cholesterol and to help protect against heart disease.

MANGO & YOGURT smoothies

1	large mango, peeled and sliced
1	cup (250 ml) low-fat vanilla yogurt
1/2	cup (120 ml) crushed ice
1/2	cup (120 ml) freshly squeezed orange juice

Serves 2 • Preparation 10 minutes • Difficulty 1

1. Place two tall glasses in the freezer to chill. Reserve 2–4 small slices of mango to garnish.

2. Combine the remaining mango, yogurt, ice, and orange juice in a blender and blend until smooth.

3. Pour into the glasses, top with the reserved slices of mango, and serve.

If you liked this recipe, you will love these as well.

MANGO & PEACH
smoothies

EXOTIC GREEN TEA
smoothies

EXOTIC FRUIT
smoothies

BANANA & NUT smoothies

2 bananas
2 cups (500 ml) low-fat vanilla yogurt
1/2 cup (60 g) chopped walnuts
1 teaspoon ground cinnamon
3 teaspoons honey
1/4 teaspoon ground nutmeg

Serves 2 • Preparation 10 minutes + 2 hours to chill • Difficulty 1

1. Peel the bananas and cut into 1-inch (2.5-cm) chunks. Chill in the freezer until solid, about 2 hours.

2. Place two tall glasses in the freezer to chill.

3. Combine the bananas, yogurt, walnuts, cinnamon, honey, and nutmeg in a blender and blend until smooth.

4. Pour into the glasses and serve.

MELON & ALMOND SMOOTHIES
with chamomile

1 cup (250 ml) almond milk (see page 56)

2 apples, peeled, cored, and chopped

2 cups (250 g) diced cantaloupe (rock) melon

¼ cup (60 g) plain yogurt

1–2 teaspoons dried chamomile flowers + extra to garnish

Serves 2 • Preparation 10 minutes • Difficulty 1

1. Place two medium glasses in the freezer to chill.

2. Combine the almond milk, apples, melon, yogurt, and chamomile flowers in a blender and blend until smooth.

3. Pour into the glasses. Garnish with the extra chamomile flowers and serve.

Raspberries are an excellent source of vitamin C and a good source of phosphorus, selenium, and dietary fiber.

CHERRY & RASPBERRY smoothies

1 cup (200 g) unsweetened frozen cherries

1 cup (200 g) fresh or frozen raspberries

1 cup (250 ml) frozen low-fat vanilla yogurt

1 cup (200 g) crushed ice

1 cup (250 ml) low-fat milk

1 teaspoon of vanilla extract (essence)

Fresh cherries to garnish

Serves 2–3 • Preparation 10 minutes • Difficulty 1

1. Place two or three glasses in the freezer to chill.

2. Blend the cherries, raspberries, yogurt, milk, ice, and vanilla extract in a blender until smooth.

3. Pour into the glasses, garnish with the fresh cherries, and serve.

If you liked this recipe, you will love these as well.

BANANA & CHERRY
smoothies

BERRY BERRY
smoothies

CHOCOLATE &
RASPBERRY smoothies

MELON & KIWI smoothies

2 cups (300 g) cubed cantaloupe (rock) melon
1 small Granny Smith apple, peeled, cored, and chopped
1 kiwi fruit, peeled and chopped
2 tablespoons honey
1 tablespoon freshly squeezed lemon juice
$^1/_2$ cup (120 ml) crushed ice

Serves 2 • Preparation 10 minutes • Difficulty 1

1. Place two medium glasses in the freezer to chill. Reserve a few cubes of melon to garnish.

2. Combine the remaining melon with the apple, kiwi fruit, honey, lemon juice, and ice in a blender and blend until smooth.

3. Pour into the glasses. Press the reserved melon cubes onto toothpicks and use them to garnish the glasses. Serve.

PAPAYA PASSION smoothies

2   papayas, peeled, seeded, and chopped

Pulp from 3 passion fruit + 1–2 tablespoons extra to garnish

2   cups (500 ml) milk

1/3 cup (90 ml) sweetened condensed milk

1   cup (250 ml) vanilla yogurt

1   cup (250 ml) crushed ice

Serves 4 • Preparation 15 minutes • Difficulty 1

1. Place four tall glasses in the freezer to chill.

2. Combine the papayas, passion fruit, milk, sweetened condensed milk, yogurt, and crushed ice in a blender and blend until smooth.

3. Pour into the chilled glasses, garnish with the extra passion fruit pulp, and serve.

This makes a lovely breakfast smoothie during the hot summer months. Chop the peaches and mango the night before and place in the freezer. In the morning you will just need to blend and serve.

MANGO & PEACH smoothie

2	peaches, pitted and sliced
1	mango, peeled and diced
1	cup (250 ml) plain low-fat yogurt
1/2	cup (120 ml) freshly squeezed orange juice

Serves 2 • Preparation 20 minutes + 4 hours to freeze • Cooking 5 minutes • Difficulty 1

1. Prepare the peaches and mango and place in the freezer until solid, at least 4 hours. This can be done the night before serving.

2. Place two tall glasses or a small pitcher (jug) in the freezer to chill. Reserve a few slices of peach and a few cubes of mango to garnish.

3. Combine the remaining peaches, mango, yogurt, and orange juice in a blender and blend until smooth.

4. Pour into the glasses or pitcher, garnish with the reserved pieces of fruit, and serve.

If you liked this recipe, you will love these as well.

BANANA & PEACH smoothies

MANGO smoothies

ORANGE FRUIT juice

APPLE & APRICOT smoothies

1	organic Granny Smith apple
1	cup (250 ml) apple juice
4	fresh or frozen apricots
1	banana
1	cup (250 ml) plain yogurt
$1/2$	cup (120 ml) crushed ice
1	tablespoon honey

Serves 2 • Preparation 10 minutes • Difficulty 1

1. Place two tall glasses in the freezer to chill. Cut the apple in half, remove the core, and cut two slices for the garnish.

2. Blend the remaining apple with the apple juice, apricots, banana, yogurt, crushed ice, and honey until smooth.

3. Pour into the glasses, garnish with the slices of apple, and serve.

CARIBBEAN smoothies

2   bananas
1   cup (250 ml) low-fat vanilla
     yogurt
1   cup (150 g) fresh pineapple
     pieces
1   cup (150 g) fresh papaya
     pieces
1/2 cup (120 ml) coconut milk
     + 1 tablespoon extra to
     garnish
4–6 ice cubes

Serves 2 • Preparation 10 minutes + 2 hours to freeze • Difficulty 1

1. Peel the bananas and cut into 1-inch (2.5-cm) chunks. Chill in the freezer until solid, about 2 hours.

2. Place two glasses in the freezer to chill. Reserve a slice or two of pineapple or papaya to garnish.

3. Combine the banana, yogurt, pineapple, papaya, coconut milk, and ice cubes in a blender and blend until smooth.

4. Pour into the glasses. Press the reserved fruit onto tooth-picks to garnish. Drizzle with the coconut milk and serve.

These smoothies contain flax seed meal. Flax seeds are a very good source of omega-3 fatty acids and insoluble fiber which help regulate cholesterol, blood glucose, and digestion. If you are not used to taking flax seeds, begin with small amounts. They are very high in fiber and can cause diarrhea and cramping.

BLUEBERRY & ALMOND smoothies

1 banana
16 whole almonds
$^1/_4$ cup (30 g) rolled oats
1 tablespoon flax seed meal + extra flax seeds to garnish (optional)
1 cup (200 g) frozen blueberries
1 cup (250 ml) raspberry yogurt
$^1/_2$ cup (120 ml) grape juice
1 cup (250 ml) buttermilk

Serves 2 • Preparation 10 minutes + 2 hours to freeze • Difficulty 1

1. Peel the banana and cut into 1-inch (2.5-cm) chunks. Chill in the freezer until solid, about 2 hours.

2. Place two glasses in the freezer to chill.

3. Combine the almonds, oats, and flax seed meal in a food processor and blend until finely ground. Add the frozen banana, frozen blueberries, yogurt, grape juice, and buttermilk and purée until smooth.

4. Pour into the glasses, garnish with the extra flax seeds, if using, and serve.

If you liked this recipe, you will love these as well.

BLUEBERRY smoothies

STRAWBERRY & BLUEBERRY smoothies

FRESH RED FRUIT smoothies

EXOTIC GREEN TEA smoothies

2 bags mint-flavored green tea
2 cups (500 ml) boiling water
1 cup (200 g) diced mango
1 cup (200 g) diced papaya
2–3 tablespoons honey
1 cup (250 ml) crushed ice
1/4 cup (60 ml) freshly squeezed lemon juice + thin slices of lemon to garnish

Serves 2 • Preparation 10 minutes + 30 minutes to cool • Difficulty 1

1. Steep the tea bags in the boiling water for 3–5 minutes. Remove and let the tea cool to room temperature.

2. Place two tall glasses in the freezer to chill.

3. Combine the tea, mango, papaya, honey, and crushed ice in a blender and blend until smooth.

4. Pour into the glasses, garnish with the lemon, and serve.

EXOTIC FRUIT smoothies

1   banana
1   small pineapple, peeled and chopped
1   papaya, peeled and chopped
1   mango, peeled and chopped
1   guava, peeled and chopped
1   cup (250 ml) cranberry juice
1   cup (250 ml) crushed ice

Serves 2–4 • Preparation 15 minutes • Difficulty 1

1. Place two to four serving glasses in the freezer to chill.

2. Reserve a few pieces of fresh fruit to garnish. Combine the remaining pineapple, papaya, mango, guava, cranberry juice, and ice in a blender and blend until smooth.

3. Pour into the glasses, garnish with the fruit, and serve.

These are very healthy smoothies and an ideal way to start the day. Pineapples are a good source of vitamins C and B6, manganese, and copper. They also contain digestive enzymes with strong anti-inflammatory properties. Wheat germ is very rich in many nutrients, especially B vitamins, while flax seeds are full of fiber and omega-3 fatty acids.

PINEAPPLE & ALMOND SMOOTHIES
with wheat germ

2	cups (350 g) fresh pineapple chunks
1	cup (250 ml) pineapple juice
1/2	cup (120 ml) almond milk (see page 56)
1	banana
2	tablespoons wheat germ
4	teaspoons flax seeds
1/2	cup (120 ml) crushed ice

Serves 2 • Preparation 10 minutes • Difficulty 1

1. Place two tall glasses in the freezer to chill. Reserve a few pineapple chunks to garnish.

2. Combine the remaining pineapple chunks, juice, almond milk, banana, wheat germ, flax seeds, and crushed ice in a blender and blend until smooth.

3. Pour into the glasses, garnish with the reserved pineapple, and serve.

If you liked this recipe, you will love these as well.

YELLOW & GREEN
layered smoothies

CARIBBEAN
smoothies

EXOTIC FRUIT
smoothies

CRANBERRY & ORANGE tofu smoothies

1 cup (180 g) dried cranberries
1/2 cup (120 ml) freshly squeezed orange juice
1/2 cup (120 g) soft tofu
2 oranges, peeled and seeds removed
2 tablespoons honey
1 tablespoon finely grated ginger

Serves 2 • Preparation 10 minutes • Difficulty 1

1. Place two tall glasses in the freezer to chill.

2. Combine the cranberries, orange juice, tofu, oranges, honey, and ginger in a blender and blend until smooth.

3. Pour into the chilled glasses and serve.

PINEAPPLE, COCONUT & PECAN smoothies

2 bananas
2 cups (500 ml) milk
1 cup (250 ml) vanilla yogurt
1/2 cup (120 ml) crushed pineapple
2 tablespoons sweetened shredded (desicated) coconut
2 tablespoons toasted chopped pecans to garnish

Serves 2–4 • Preparation 15 minutes + 2 hours to chill • Difficulty 1

1. Peel the bananas and cut into 1-inch (2.5-cm) chunks. Chill in the freezer until solid, about 2 hours.

2. Place two to four glasses in the freezer to chill.

3. Combine the frozen banana, milk, yogurt, pineapple, and coconut in a blender and blend until smooth.

4. Pour into the glasses, sprinkle with the pecans, and serve.

Blueberries and strawberries together are a great health combo. Many scientific studies have suggested that these berries can help protect against several different types of cancer, improve cognitive abilities in the elderly, and cut rates of heart disease.

STRAWBERRY & BLUEBERRY smoothies

1	large banana
1	cup (150 g) sliced fresh strawberries
1/2	cup (75 g) fresh blueberries + extra to garnish
1	cup (250 ml) milk
1/2	cup (120 ml) vanilla yogurt
1/2	cup (120 ml) crushed ice
1	teaspoon vanilla extract (essence)

Serves 2 • Preparation 10 minutes • Difficulty 1

1. Place two tall glasses in the freezer to chill.

2. Combine the banana, strawberries, blueberries, milk, yogurt, ice, and vanilla in a blender and blend until smooth.

3. Pour into glasses, garnish with the extra blueberries, and serve.

If you liked this recipe, you will love these as well.

FRESH RED FRUIT
smoothies

STRAWBERRY & OATMEAL
breakfast smoothies

STRAWBERRY
smoothies

FRESH RED FRUIT smoothies

$\frac{1}{2}$ cup (75 g) fresh blueberries

$\frac{1}{2}$ cup (75 g) fresh raspberries + extra to garnish

$\frac{1}{2}$ cup (75 g) fresh sliced strawberries

$\frac{1}{3}$ cup (90 ml) pomegranate juice

$\frac{1}{3}$ cup (90 ml) mango juice

1   cup (250 ml) skimmed milk

2   tablespoons honey

Serves 2 • Preparation 10 minutes • Difficulty 1

1. Place two tall glasses in the freezer to chill.

2. Combine the blueberries, raspberries, strawberries, pomegranate juice, mango juice, milk, and honey in a blender and blend until smooth.

3. Pour into the chilled glasses, garnish with the raspberries, and serve.

STRAWBERRY & OATMEAL breakfast smoothies

1   banana, peeled and chopped

15   large fresh strawberries, cleaned

$1^1/_2$ cups (375 ml) soy milk

$^1/_2$ cup (60 g) rolled oats

2   teaspoons honey

$^1/_2$ teaspoon vanilla extract (essence)

     Few slices of banana and strawberries to garnish

Serves 2 • Preparation 15 minutes + 12 hours to freeze • Difficulty 1

1. Put the banana and strawberries in the freezer the night before to freeze.

2. Place two tall glasses in the freezer to chill.

3. Combine the frozen banana, strawberries, soy milk, rolled oats, honey, and vanilla extract in a blender and blend until smooth.

4. Pour into the glasses, garnish with the bananas and strawberries, and serve.

SPICED PEAR smoothies

Serves 2 • Preparation 10 minutes • Difficulty 1

2	large pears, peeled, cored, and quartered	$1/2$	teaspoon ground cinnamon + extra to dust
1	banana		
1	cup (250 ml) milk	$1/8$	teaspoon ground nutmeg
$1/2$	cup (120 ml) vanilla yogurt	1	tablespoon raw sugar

1. Place two glasses in the freezer to chill.

2. Combine the pears, banana, milk, yogurt, cinnamon, and nutmeg in a blender and blend until smooth.

3. Pour into the glasses. Sprinkle with the raw sugar, dust with extra cinnamon, and serve.

PEANUT BUTTER smoothies

Serves 2 • Preparation 10 minutes • Difficulty 1

2	cups (500 ml) plain soy milk	4	tablespoons peanut butter
2	bananas		

1. Place two glasses in the freezer to chill. Reserve 2–3 slices of banana to garnish.

2. Combine the soy milk, banana, and peanut butter in a blender and blend until smooth.

3. Pour into the glasses, garnish with the banana, and serve.

STRAWBERRY smoothies

Serves 2–4 • Preparation 10 minutes • Difficulty 1

2	cups (300 g) fresh strawberries	1	cup (250 ml) frozen vanilla yogurt
2	bananas		
1	cup (250 ml) pineapple juice		

1. Place two to four tall glasses in the freezer to chill. Reserve a few whole strawberries to garnish.

2. Combine the remaining strawberries, bananas, pineapple juice, and yogurt in a blender and blend until smooth.

3. Pour into the glasses. Garnish each one by pressing a whole strawberry onto the side of the glass.

MANGO smoothies

Serves 2–4 • Preparation 10 minutes • Difficulty 1

1	pound (500 g) fresh or frozen mango chunks	1	cup (250 ml) coconut milk
$1/3$	cup (90 ml) freshly squeezed lime juice	$1/4$	cup (60 g) thick Greek-style yogurt
		10	ice cubes

1. Place two to four tall glasses in the freezer to chill.

2. Combine the mango, coconut milk, lime juice, yogurt, and ice in a blender and blend until smooth.

3. Pour into the chilled glasses and serve.

veggie smoothies

CARROT & LIME SMOOTHIES with cilantro

1   cup (250 ml) freshly squeezed
    orange juice
1   cup (200 g) cooked sliced
    carrots
    Freshly squeezed juice of
    1 lime + wedges to garnish
$^1/_2$ cup (120 g) plain yogurt
4-6   ice cubes
    Fresh cilantro (coriander)
    leaves to garnish

Serves 2 • Preparation 10 minutes • Difficulty 1

1. Place two glasses in the freezer to chill.

2. Combine the orange juice, carrots, lime juice, yogurt, and ice cubes in a blender and blend until smooth.

3. Pour into the glasses, garnish with the wedges of lime and the cilantro, and serve.

If you liked this recipe, you will love these as well.

44

CARROT, APPLE
& CUCUMBER smoothies

50

PEA & CARROT
smoothies

56

CILANTRO & ALMOND
detox smoothies

Don't let your smoothies sit around after they are blended; serve them straight up while the precious nutrients they contain are fresh and zippy. We have suggested that you chill the glasses before filling them. This will make the smoothies taste even more deliciously fresh.

CARROT, APPLE & CUCUMBER smoothies

1 large cucumber, peeled
4 carrots, cut in chunks
1 cup (250 ml) apple juice
2 tablespoons freshly squeezed lemon juice

Serves 2 • Preparation 10 minutes • Difficulty 1

1. Place two glasses in the freezer to chill. Reserve a few slices of cucumber, with peel, to garnish and nibble with the drinks.

2. Combine the carrots, cucumber, apple juice, and lemon juice in a blender and blend until smooth.

3. Pour into the glasses, garnish with the slices of cucumber, and serve.

If you liked this recipe, you will love these as well.

43

CARROT & LIME
SMOOTHIES with cilantro

94

CARROT, APPLE
& CELERY juice

96

SWEET POTATO, CARROT
& APPLE juice

CUCUMBER & TOMATO SMOOTHIES with tabasco

1 small cucumber, peeled and chopped + extra cucumber sticks to serve

1 cup (250 ml) tomato juice

1-2 teaspoons Worcestershire sauce

4-6 drops Tabasco sauce

$\frac{1}{2}$ cup (120 ml) crushed ice

2 stalks celery to serve
   Hot paprika, to dust

Serves 2 • Preparation 10 minutes • Difficulty 1

1. Place two glasses in the freezer to chill.

2. Combine the cucumber, tomato juice, Worcestershire sauce, Tabasco, and ice in a blender and blend until smooth.

3. Pour into the glasses, garnish with the celery sticks, and dust with the paprika. Serve at once.

CELERY & SOY SMOOTHIES with spices

1   cup (250 ml) soy milk
4   stalks celery + 2 extra to serve
4   tablespoons chopped celeriac
2   tomatoes
1   teaspoon curry powder
$\frac{1}{2}$ teaspoon turmeric
$\frac{1}{4}$ teaspoon ground cumin

Serves 2 • Preparation 10 minutes • Difficulty 1

1. Place two glasses in the freezer to chill.

2. Combine the soy milk, celery, celeriac, tomato, curry powder, turmeric, and cumin in a blender and blend until smooth.

3. Pour into the glasses and serve garnished with the extra celery stalks.

Beets, also known as beetroot or red beet, are highly nutritious and healthy root vegetables. They contain unique pigment antioxidants that are believed to offer protection against coronary heart disease and stroke and to lower cholesterol levels.

BEET & APPLE smoothies

14	ounces (400 g) cooked beets (beetroot)
2	apples, peeled, cored and chopped
$1/2$	cup (120 ml) apple juice
2	stalks celery, chopped
1	tablespoon balsamic vinegar
1	teaspoon finely grated ginger
1	clove garlic
1-2	tablespoons sour cream to garnish

Serves 4 • Preparation 15 minutes • Difficulty 1

1. Place four glasses in the freezer to chill.

2. Chop 1–2 tablespoons of beets into tiny cubes and set aside to garnish.

3. Combine the beets, apples, apple juice, celery, balsamic vinegar, ginger, and garlic in a blender and blend until smooth.

4. Pour into glasses, top with the sour cream and pieces of beet, and serve.

If you liked this recipe, you will love these as well.

GREEN APPLE
& CELERY juice

APPLE & GINGER
juice

CABBAGE & APPLE
JUICE with strawberries

PARSLEY & LEMON smoothies

Serves 2 • Preparation 10 minutes • Difficulty 1

2	lemons, peeled and seeded	2	bananas
2	cups (100 g) fresh flat-leaf parsley, tough stalks removed	2–3	tablespoons honey
		2	cups (500 ml) crushed ice

1. Place two large glasses in the freezer to chill.
2. Combine the parsley, lemon, bananas, honey, and ice in a blender and blend until smooth.
3. Pour into the glasses and serve.

PEA & CARROT smoothies

Serves 2 • Preparation 10 minutes • Difficulty 1

2	cups (300 g) cooked peas	1/2	cup (120 ml) plain yogurt
1	cup (150 g) chopped cooked carrots	1	tablespoon chopped fresh mint
1/2	cup (120 g) applesauce		
1	cup (250 ml) apple juice		

1. Combine the peas, carrots, applesauce, apple juice, yogurt, and mint in a blender and blend until smooth.
2. Pour into two glasses and serve.

PUMPKIN & APRICOT smoothies

Serves 2 • Preparation 15 minutes • Cooking 5 minutes Difficulty 1

1	cup (200 g) pumpkin purée (canned or freshly steamed at home and mashed)	1/2	teaspoon ground cinnamon + extra to dust
1	cup (180 g) chopped apricots, fresh or canned	1/4	teaspoon ground nutmeg
1	tablespoon honey	1	cup (250 ml) crushed ice
1 1/4	cups (300 ml) low-fat milk		

1. Place two tall glasses in the freezer to chill.
2. Combine the pumpkin purée, apricots, honey, milk, cinnamon, nutmeg, and ice in a blender and blend until smooth.
3. Pour into the glasses, dust with a little extra cinnamon, and serve.

SPINACH & BERRY smoothies

Serves 2 • Preparation 10 minutes • Difficulty 1

2	cups (300 g) fresh or frozen blueberries	1	cup (250 ml) plain yogurt
1	cup (50 g) fresh spinach leaves	1/2	cup (120 ml) milk
		1	tablespoon honey

1. Place two glasses in the freezer to chill. Reserve a few whole blueberries to garnish.
2. Combine the remaining blueberries, spinach, yogurt, milk, and honey in a blender and blend until smooth.
3. Pour into the glasses, sprinkle the reserved blueberries on top, and serve.

These delicious and nutritious smoothies fall somewhere between a soup and a smoothie. Serve them during the winter months.

WARM ONION, CELERY & PARSNIP smoothies

1^1/$_2$ cups (375 ml) milk
2 onions, quartered
2 stalks celery, cut into chunks
1 parsnip, cut into chunks
^{1}/$_2$ teaspoon star anise
+ whole star anise to garnish

Serves 2-4 • Preparation 15 minutes • Cooking 10–15 minutes • Difficulty 1

1. Bring the milk to a boil in a medium saucepan. Add the onions, celery, and parsnip and simmer until the vegetables are tender, 10–15 minutes.

2. Pour the milk mixture and star anise into a blender and blend until smooth.

3. Pour into heatproof glasses and garnish with the star anise. Serve warm.

If you liked this recipe, you will love these as well.

CELERY & SOY
smoothies

TOMATO & CELERY
smoothies

SPICY VEGGIE
smoothies

FENNEL & ORANGE smoothies

1   bulb fennel, tough outer leaves removed
2   oranges, peeled and seeded
1   cup (50 g) baby spinach leaves
$^1/_2$ cup (120 ml) crushed ice

Serves 2 • Preparation 10 minutes • Difficulty 1

1. Place two tall glasses in the freezer to chill.

2. Combine the fennel, oranges, spinach, and ice in a blender and blend until smooth.

3. Pour into the glasses and serve.

TOMATO smoothies

6	medium ripe tomatoes
1	cup (250 ml) tomato juice
1/2	cup (120 ml) apple juice
2	small carrots, chopped
2	stalks celery
1	cup (250 ml) crushed ice
	Celery stalks to serve
	Carrot sticks to serve

Serves 2 • Preparation 10 minutes • Difficulty 1

1. Place two serving glasses in the freezer to chill.

2. Combine the tomatoes, tomato juice, apple juice, carrot, celery, and ice in a blender and blend until smooth.

3. Pour into the glasses and serve with the carrots and celery.

CILANTRO & ALMOND detox smoothies

Almond Milk

1   cup (150 g) raw unsalted almonds

4   cups (1 liter) filtered or spring water

1   teaspoon vanilla extract (essence)

Smoothies

$1/2$ cup (120 ml) coconut milk (fresh or canned)

1   papaya, pitted and chopped

1   cup (50 g) fresh cilantro leaves

6   fresh strawberries + extra to garnish

4   dates, pitted

Serves 1–2 • Preparation 15 minutes + 8–12 hours to soak • Difficulty 1

Almond Milk

1. Soak the almonds for 8–12 hours in 1 cup (250 ml) of water. Drain well, discarding the water.

2. Transfer to a blender. Add the remaining 3 cups (750 ml) of water and the vanilla and blend until smooth and well mixed. Strain through a fine-mesh sieve.

Smoothies

1. Place one or two tall glasses in the freezer to chill.

2. Blend 1 cup (250 ml) of almond milk with the coconut milk, papaya, cilantro, strawberries, and dates until smooth.

3. Pour into the glasses, garnish with the extra strawberries, and serve.

If you liked this recipe, you will love these as well.

CARROT & LIME SMOOTHIES with cilantro

PARSLEY & LEMON smoothies

FENNEL & ORANGE smoothies

AVOCADO smoothies

2 cups (500 ml) almond milk (see page 56)

1 avocado, peeled and chopped

1/2 cup (120 ml) crushed ice

Freshly squeezed juice of 1 lime + 2 slices of lime to garnish

2-3 tablespoons sweetened condensed milk

Hot paprika, to dust

Serves 2 • Preparation 10 minutes • Difficulty 1

1. Place two tall glasses in the freezer to chill.

2. Combine the almond milk, avocado, ice, lime juice, and sweetened condensed milk in a blender and blend until smooth.

3. Pour into the glasses. Garnish with the lime, dust with the paprika, and serve.

GREEN smoothies

1 banana
1 crisp green organic eating apple, cored and chopped
1 cup (150 g) seedless white grapes
1 cup (250 ml) low-fat plain yogurt
2 cups (100 g) fresh baby spinach leaves

Serves 2 • Preparation 5–10 minutes • Difficulty 1

1. Place two tall glasses in the freezer to chill. Reserve a few pieces of fruit to garnish.

2. Combine the remaining banana, apple, grapes, yogurt, and spinach in a blender and blend until smooth.

3. Pour into the glasses. Press the reserved fruit onto toothpicks and use to garnish the drinks. Serve.

TOMATO & CELERY SMOOTHIES
with fresh herbs

¹/₂	cup (25 g) fresh parsley leaves
¹/₂	cup (25 g) fresh mint leaves
¹/₂	cup (25 g) fresh cilantro (coriander) leaves
1	pound (500 g) tomatoes, peeled, seeded and coarsely chopped
¹/₂	cup (120 ml) carrot juice
1	tablespoon freshly squeezed lemon juice
4	stalks celery stalks, trimmed and sliced
4	scallions (green onions), trimmed and roughly chopped

Serves 2-4 • Preparation 15 minutes • Difficulty 1

1. Place two to four serving glasses in the freezer to chill.

2. Reserve 2–3 leaves from each of the fresh herbs to garnish.

3. Combine the tomatoes, carrot juice, and lemon juice in a blender and blend until well mixed. Add the celery, scallions, parsley, mint, and cilantro and blend until smooth.

4. Pour into the glasses, garnish with the reserved herbs, and serve.

If you liked this recipe, you will love these as well.

TOMATO smoothies

SPICY VEGGIE smoothies

HOMEMADE TOMATO juice

SPICY VEGGIE smoothies

6	medium vine tomatoes
2	red bell peppers (capsicums)
1	zucchini (courgette)
1/2	white onion
1	clove garlic
6	stalks celery
1	teaspoon flax seeds
1	tablespoon dulse flakes
1	fresh red chile (or to taste)
1/2	teaspoon hot paprika + extra to dust
1/2	avocado

Serves 2 • Preparation 10 minutes • Difficulty 1

1. Place two tall glasses in the freezer to chill.

2. Put the tomatoes in a blender and blend until chopped. Add the bell peppers, zucchini, onion, garlic, celery, flax seeds, dulse flakes, chile, paprika, and avocado and blend until smooth.

3. Pour into glasses, dust with paprika, and serve.

SPINACH & PEAR smoothies

4   medium, sweet, ripe pears

4   cups (200 g) baby spinach
leaves

Serves 2 • Preparation 10 minutes • Difficulty 1

1. Place two tall glasses in the freezer to chill.

2. Combine the pears with the spinach in a blender and blend until smooth.

3. Pour into the glasses and serve.

dessert smoothies

FRUIT & ORANGE LIQUEUR smoothies

1 cup (250 ml) orange liqueur, such as Grand Marnier

$^1/_2$ cup (100 g) sugar

2 cups (300 g) frozen raspberries

2 cups (500 ml) milk

1 cup (150 g) frozen cranberries

$^1/_2$ cup (120 ml) vodka

2 tablespoons honey

3 cups (750 ml) vanilla or white chocolate ice cream + a little extra, softened, to top

Edible flowers to garnish (optional)

Serves 6 • Preparation: 20 minutes • Difficulty 2

1. Moisten the edges of six brandy snifters with orange liqueur. Place the sugar in a saucer and dip the brandy glasses in the sugar so that they are coated with a rim of sugar crystals. Place in the freezer carefully.

2. Combine the raspberries, milk, cranberries, remaining orange liqueur, vodka, honey, and ice cream in a blender and blend until smooth.

3. Pour into the prepared glasses, taking care not to knock the sugar off the rims. Top each one with a teaspoon or so of ice cream and a few tiny edible flowers, if desired.

If you liked this recipe, you will love these as well.

BERRY BERRY smoothies

BANANA & STRAWBERRY smoothies

BLUEBERRY & CREAM CHEESE smoothies

The berries and ice cream blend with the milk to make a lovely, creamy dessert. Serve with long-handled spoons to scoop out the fruit. You can vary the berries too according to what you have on hand. Black currants, red currants, strawberries, boysenberries, and cranberries will all work well.

BERRY BERRY smoothies

2	scoops vanilla ice cream
1	cup (200 g) frozen blackberries
1	cup (200 g) frozen raspberries
1	cup (200 g) frozen blueberries
1$^1/_2$	cups (375 ml) milk
1	teaspoon freshly squeezed lime juice
	A few fresh berries to garnish

Serves 2 • Preparation 10 minutes • Difficulty 1

1. Place two large glasses in the freezer to chill.

2. Combine the ice cream, blackberries, raspberries, blueberries, milk, and lime juice in a blender and blend until smooth.

3. Pour into the glasses. Drop a few fresh berries in to garnish and serve.

If you liked this recipe, you will love these as well.

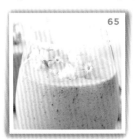
65

FRUIT & ORANGE LIQUEUR smoothies

74

CHOCOLATE & RASPBERRY smoothies

80

RASPBERRY & WHITE CHOCOLATE smoussies

MOCHA BANANA smoothies

2 bananas
2 scoops chocolate ice cream
1¹/₂ cups (375 ml) milk
¹/₂ cup (120 g) crushed ice
2 teaspoons freeze-dried coffee granules
2 tablespoons chocolate syrup

Serves 1 • Preparation 5 minutes • Difficulty 1

1. Place two tall glasses in the freezer to chill.

2. Combine the bananas, ice cream, ice, and coffee in a blender and blend until smooth.

3. Pour into the glasses, drizzle with the chocolate syrup, and serve.

CHOCOLATE AFTER-DINNER smoothies

4   scoops chocolate ice cream
$1/4$ cup (60 ml) dark rum
1   tablespoon kahlua
1   tablespoon amaretto
      (almond liqueur)
1   cup (250 ml) crushed ice
      Whipped cream to garnish
      Chocolate shavings to garnish

Serves 2-4 • Preparation 10 minutes • Difficulty 1

1. Place two to four glasses in the freezer to chill.

2. Combine the ice cream, rum, kahlua, amaretto, and ice in a blender and blend until smooth.

3. Pour into the glasses, top with a dollop of cream and some chocolate shavings, and serve.

69

Be sure to choose the right glasses for these eyecatching smoothies. You will need tall glasses with plenty of space to squirt the chocolate sauce. This is a quick way to whip up dessert for unexpected guests.

BANANA SMOOTHIES
with chocolate & nuts

4	tablespoons chocolate syrup
1	banana
$1^1/_2$	cups (375 ml) milk
1	scoop vanilla ice cream + 2 heaped teaspoons to garnish
1	tablespoon honey
1	square dark chocolate, grated
1	tablespoon mixed chopped nuts

Serves 2 • Preparation 10 minutes • Difficulty 1

1. Squirt 1 tablespoon of chocolate syrup inside each glass, creating a pretty pattern. Put the glasses in the freezer to chill the syrup in place.

2. Combine the banana, milk, ice cream, and honey in a blender and blend until smooth.

3. Pour into the glasses. Top each one with a teaspoon of softened ice cream, some chopped nuts, grated chocolate, and a squirt of the remaining chocolate syrup. Serve immediately.

If you liked this recipe, you will love these as well.

MOCHA BANANA smoothies

CHOCOLATE AFTER-DINNER smoothies

BANANA SPLIT smoothies

CHERRY smoothies

Serves 2 • Preparation 10 minutes + 2 hours to chill
Difficulty 1

1	banana	1¹/₂	cups (375 ml) apple juice
1¹/₂	cups (350 g) frozen cherries	2	teaspoons vanilla extract (essence)
1	cup (250 ml) vanilla ice cream		

1. Peel the banana and cut into 1-inch (2.5-cm) chunks. Chill in the freezer until solid, about 2 hours.

2. Place two tall glasses in the freezer to chill.

3. Combine the banana, cherries, ice cream, apple juice, and vanilla in a blender and blend until smooth.

4. Pour into the glasses and serve.

BANANA SPLIT smoothies

Serves 2–4 • Preparation 10 minutes • Difficulty 1

2	bananas	8	ice cubes
1	cup (250 g) crushed pineapple	1	scoop vanilla ice cream
1¹/₂	cups (375 ml) milk	¹/₂	cup (120 ml) heavy (double) cream
6	fresh strawberries		Chocolate syrup
2	tablespoons honey		Maraschino cherries

1. Place two to four glasses in the freezer to chill.

2. Combine the bananas, pineapple, milk, strawberries, and honey in a blender and blend until smooth. Add the ice and ice cream and blend until slushy.

3. Pour the smoothies into the glasses.

4. Beat the cream until thickened and spoon over the top. Drizzle with chocolate syrup and top each glass with 1–2 maraschino cherries.

PUMPKIN & SPICE smoothies

Serves 4 • Preparation 10 minutes • Difficulty 1

6	ounces (180 g) cream cheese, softened	¹/₂	teaspoon pumpkin pie spice or allspice + extra to dust
1	(15-ounce/400-g) can pumpkin purée, chilled	1¹/₂	cups (375 ml) milk
1	cup (250 g) vanilla yogurt	6	ice cubes
¹/₃	cup (75 g) firmly packed dark brown sugar		Whipped cream
1¹/₂	cups (350 g) vanilla ice cream		Lingue de chat (cat tongue cookies) or other vanilla cookies to serve

1. Place four tall glasses in the freezer to chill.

2. Combine the cream cheese, pumpkin, yogurt, brown sugar, ice cream, spice, milk, and ice cubes in a blender and blend until smooth.

3. Pour into the glasses. Top with whipped cream and dust each one with extra pumpkin pie spice. Serve with the cookies.

COFFEE smoothies

Serves 2 • Preparation 10 minutes • Difficulty 1

2	teaspoons instant coffee granules	2	teaspoons sugar
1¹/₂	cups (375 ml) milk	4	ice cubes
1	teaspoon vanilla extract (essence)		Whipped cream
			Chocolate shavings

1. Place two glasses in the freezer to chill.

2. Combine the coffee granules, milk, vanilla, and sugar in a blender and blend until smooth.

3. Put 2 ice cubes in each glass and pour the smoothie in over the top. Garnish each glass with a dollop of whipped cream and a scattering of chocolate shavings and serve.

CHOCOLATE & RASPBERRY SMOOTHIES
with fresh mint

1   cup (250 ml) chocolate milk
2   scoops chocolate ice cream
1¹/₂   cups (250 g) fresh raspberries
       + extra to garnish
1   small banana
       Sprigs of fresh mint to serve

Serves 2 • Preparation 10 minutes • Difficulty 1

1. Place two tall glasses in the freezer to chill.

2. Combine the chocolate milk, ice cream, raspberries, and banana in a blender and blend until smooth.

3. Pour into the glasses, garnish with the sprigs of mint, and serve.

BANANA & STRAWBERRY SMOOTHIES
with chocolate & cream

2 cups (300 g) fresh strawberries

2 bananas

1 cup (250 ml) pineapple juice

1 cup (250 ml) frozen vanilla yogurt

Chocolate syrup to garnish

Serves 2 • Preparation 10 minutes • Difficulty 1

1. Place two glasses in the freezer to chill. Slice two strawberries to garnish and set aside. Reserve 2 teaspoons of yogurt to garnish.

2. Combine the remaining strawberries, bananas, pineapple juice, and yogurt in a blender and blend until smooth.

3. Pour into the glasses, garnish with the strawberries, yogurt, and chocolate syrup, and serve.

These smoothies get their lovely pale violet-blue color from the mixture of blueberries and cream cheese. If you use raspberries instead of blueberries you will get striking pale pink smoothies.

76

BLUEBERRY & CREAM CHEESE smoothies

2	cups (500 ml) milk
1	cup (250 ml) vanilla frozen yogurt
1	cup (250 ml) fresh or frozen blueberries
$^1/_2$	cup (125 g) cream cheese
1	tablespoon sugar
2–4	tablespoons graham cracker crumbs (or crumbled digestive biscuits) to garnish

Serves 2–4 • Preparation 10 minutes • Difficulty 1

1. Place two to four glasses in the freezer to chill.

2. Blend the milk, yogurt, blueberries, cream cheese, and sugar in a blender and blend until smooth.

3. Pour into the glasses, sprinkle with the crumbled cookies, and serve.

If you liked this recipe, you will love these as well.

SOY & BERRYFRUIT
smoothies

BLUEBERRY & ALMOND
smoothies

BERRY BERRY
smoothies

APPLE & PUMPKIN PIE smoothies

1½ cups (350 g) vanilla ice cream
½ cup (120 g) pumpkin pie filling
1 banana, broken into chunks
2 cups (500 ml) apple juice
1 teaspoon ground cinnamon
⅛ teaspoon ground nutmeg
Wedges of Granny Smith apple to serve

Serves 2–4 • Preparation 10 minutes • Difficulty 1

1. Place two to four glasses in the freezer to chill.

2. Combine the ice cream, pumpkin pie filling, banana, apple juice, cinnamon, and nutmeg in a blender and blend until smooth.

3. Pour into the glasses and serve with the slices of apple.

PUMPKIN PIE smoothies

½ cup (120 ml) coconut milk
½ cup (120 ml) water
2 cups (400 g) cooked mashed pumpkin
1 tablespoon dark brown sugar + extra to garnish
1 teaspoon ground cinnamon
½ teaspoon ground ginger
¼ teaspoon ground nutmeg
1 teaspoon vanilla extract (essence)
12 ice cubes

Serves 2 • Preparation 10 minutes • Difficulty 1

1. Place two glasses in the freezer to chill.

2. Combine the coconut milk, water, pumpkin, brown sugar, cinnamon, ginger, nutmeg, and vanilla in a blender and blend until smooth. Add the ice and blend again.

3. Pour into the glasses, sprinkle with a little extra brown sugar, and serve.

A smoussie is what you get when you cross a smoothie with a mousse. To vary this recipe, substitute the white chocolate with the same amount of milk or dark chocolate.

RASPBERRY & WHITE CHOCOLATE smoussies

12	ounces (350 g) fresh or frozen raspberries + extra fresh to garnish
2	tablespoons sugar
2	tablespoons Grand Marnier or other orange liqueur
8	ounces (250 g) white chocolate
2	cups (500 ml) heavy (double) cream

Serves 6 • Preparation 20 minutes • Cooking 10 minutes • Difficulty 2

1. Place six small dessert glasses in the freezer to chill.

2. Blend the raspberries, sugar, and orange liqueur in a blender until smooth. Press through a fine-mesh sieve to remove the seeds. You should have about 1 cup (250 ml) of sauce.

3. Melt the chocolate and $1/2$ cup (120 ml) of cream in a double boiler over barely simmering water. Set aside to cool. Stir in 2 tablespoons of raspberry sauce.

4. Beat the remaining $1^{1}/_{2}$ cups (375 ml) of cream until thickened. Fold one-third of the cream into cooled chocolate mixture. Fold in the remaining cream.

5. Spoon the chocolate mixture into the glasses alternately with the raspberry sauce. Garnish with fresh raspberries and serve.

If you liked this recipe, you will love these as well.

FRUIT & ORANGE LIQUEUR smoothies

BANANA & STRAWBERRY smoothies

BLUEBERRY & CREAM CHEESE smoothies

CARAMEL BANANA smoothies

2   bananas
1   cup (250 g) vanilla yogurt,
1   cup (250 ml) vanilla soy milk
½   teaspoon ground cinnamon
2–3 tablespoons caramel topping

Serves 2 • Preparation 10 minutes + 2 hours to chill • Difficulty 1

1. Peel the bananas and cut into 1-inch (2.5-cm) chunks. Chill in the freezer until solid, about 2 hours.

2. Place two glasses in the freezer to chill.

3. Combine the bananas, yogurt, soy milk, and cinnamon in a blender and blender until smooth.

4. Pour into the glasses, drizzle with the caramel topping, and serve.

CHOCOLATE MINT smoothies

2 cups (500 ml) milk

2 cups (500 g) vanilla ice cream

4 tablespoons sweetened cocoa powder (instant cocoa powder)

1 teaspoon vanilla extract (essence)

$1/2$ teaspoon peppermint extract (essence)

Fresh mint sprigs to garnish

Serves 2–4 • Preparation 5–10 minutes • Difficulty 1

1. Place two to four glasses in the freezer to chill.

2. Combine the milk, ice cream, cocoa powder, and vanilla and peppermint extracts in a blender and blend until smooth.

3. Pour into the glasses, garnish with the mint, and serve.

WATERMELON & CRANBERRY soy smoothies

2   bananas

3   cups (400 g) chopped
       watermelon, seeds removed

1   cup (250 ml) cranberry juice

2   scoops vanilla soymilk ice
       cream

       Soy milk whipped cream to
       garnish

Serves 2–4 • Preparation 10 minutes + 2 hours to freeze • Difficulty 1

1. Peel the bananas and cut into 1-inch (2.5-cm) chunks.
   Chill in the freezer until solid, about 2 hours.

2. Place two to four glasses in the freezer to chill. If liked,
   reserve a few small cubes of watermelon to garnish
   the smoothies.

3. Combine the bananas, remaining watermelon, cranberry
   juice, and ice cream in a blender and blend until smooth.

4. Pour into the glasses, top with whipped cream and
   reserved watermelon cubes, if using, and serve.

If you liked this recipe, you will love these as well.

SOY & BERRYFRUIT
smoothies

STRAWBERRY & OATMEAL
breakfast smoothies

CHERRY
smoothies

CAPPUCCINO smoothies

1 cup (250 ml) very strong black coffee

1 cup (250 ml) milk

2 scoops vanilla ice cream

1 tablespoons freeze-dried coffee granules

1 teaspoon vanilla extract (essence)

$1/3$ cup (90 ml) heavy (double) cream

Coffee beans to garnish

Serves 2 • Preparation 10 minutes • Difficulty 1

1. Place two tall glasses in the freezer to chill.

2. Combine the coffee, milk, ice cream, and coffee granules in a blender and blend until smooth.

3. Beat the cream in a small bowl until thickened.

4. Pour the smoothies into the chilled glasses. Spoon the cream over the top to create a cappuccino-like topping. Decorate with the coffee beans.

DOUBLE CHOCOLATE AZTEC smoothies

2 scoops dark chocolate ice cream

1½ cups (375 ml) milk

¼ cup (60 ml) chocolate syrup

½ teaspoon crumbled dried chiles + extra to garnish

½ cup (120 ml) crushed ice

Whipped cream to garnish

Chocolate shavings to garnish

Serves 2 • Preparation 10 minutes • Difficulty 1

1. Place two glasses in the freezer to chill.

2. Combine the ice cream, milk, chocolate syrup, chiles, and crushed ice in a blender and blend until smooth.

3. Pour into the glasses and top with whipped cream and chocolate shavings. Dust with a little extra chile and serve.

These delicious smoothies are simple and quick to make and very versatile. You can whip them up and serve to finish a family meal just as easily as you can serve them at the end of a dunner party. They are perfect for every occasion!

CHOCOLATE CAPPUCCINO smoothies

4	ice cubes
1¹/₂	cups (375 ml) strong black coffee, cooled
1	cup (250 ml) heavy (double) cream
1	cup (250 ml) vanilla frozen yogurt
4	tablespoons chocolate syrup
	Chocolate-coated coffee beans

Serves 2 • Preparation 10 minutes • Difficulty 1

1. Place two glasses in the freezer to chill.

2. Put two ice cubes in each glass and pour the coffee in on top.

3. Combine the cream, frozen yogurt, and chocolate in a blender and blend until smooth.

4. Pour into the glasses over the coffee. Top with chocolate-coated coffee beans and serve.

If you liked this recipe, you will love these as well.

BANANA SMOOTHIES
with chocolate & nuts

CAPPUCCINO
smoothies

**DOUBLE CHOCOLATE
AZTEC** smoothies

AVOCADO JUICE with wasabi

$1/2$	iceberg lettuce
2	limes, peeled
1	small cucumber, peeled and seeded
1	avocado, peeled and pitted
2	teaspoons wasabi
8-10	ice cubes

Serves 2 • Preparation 10 minutes • Difficulty 1

1. Juice the lettuce, limes, and cucumber into a pitcher (jug).

2. Reserve a few small cubes of avocado. Combine the remaining avocado with the juice and wasabi in a blender and blend until smooth.

3. Place the ice cubes in two medium glasses and pour the avocado mixture in over the top. Top with the reserved cubes of avocado and serve.

If you liked this recipe, you will love these as well.

AVOCADO
smoothies

SPICY VEGGIE
smoothies

GRAPE & CUCUMBER
juice

Tests have shown time and again that conventionally grown fruit and vegetables often have detectable pesticide residues. All fresh fruit and vegetables should always be thoroughly washed. Never eat the peel or zest of conventionally grown produce. We suggest that you use organic fruit and vegetables for all the recipes in this book, but we have only specified organic when the ingredients include unpeeled fruit or zest.

GREEN APPLE & CELERY juice

4 organic Granny Smith apples
6-7 stalks celery
$^1/_2$ lemon, peeled and seeded

Serves 1-2 • Preparation: 10 minutes • Difficulty 1

1. Juice the apples, 5 stalks of celery, and the lemon into a pitcher (jug).

2. Pour the juice into one or two glasses and serve with the extra stalk of celery to munch on while you sip.

If you liked this recipe, you will love these as well.

GREEN smoothies

CARROT, APPLE
& CELERY juice

SWEET POTATO, CARROT
& APPLE juice

CARROT, APPLE & CELERY JUICE
with garlic, ginger & lemon

2 carrots
2 stalks celery
1 organic apple, cored
1 clove garlic
1 ($\frac{1}{2}$-inch/1-cm) piece ginger
$\frac{1}{2}$ lemon

Serves 1 • Preparation 10 minutes • Difficulty 1

1. Juice the carrots, celery, apple, garlic, ginger, and lemon into a pitcher (jug).

2. Pour into a glass and serve.

SALSA juice

½   lime
2   large tomatoes
1   fresh jalapeno chile
1   small onion
½   cup (25 g) fresh cilantro
      (coriander) leaves

Serves 1 • Preparation 15 minutes• Difficulty 1

1. Cut a very thin slice of lime to garnish.

2. Juice the tomatoes, chile, onion, cilantro, and lime into a pitcher (jug).

3. Pour the juice into a glass, top with the lime, and serve.

Dulse powder is made by finely grinding a type of red seaweed. It is very rich in nutrients and has a distinctive flavor. Dulse powder can be used instead of salt to flavor juices, soups, salads, and stir-fries.

SWEET POTATO, CARROT & APPLE juice

2	carrots
2	organic apples, cored
1	sweet potato
$\frac{1}{2}$	small red onion
$\frac{1}{8}$	teaspoon dulse powder

Serves 2 • Preparation 10 minutes • Difficulty 1

1. Juice the carrots, apples, sweet potato, onion, and dulse powder into a pitcher (jug).

2. Pour into two glasses and serve.

If you liked this recipe, you will love these as well.

CARROT, APPLE
& CUCUMBER smoothies

CARROT, APPLE
& CELERY juice

ORANGE, CELERY &
SWEET POTATO juice

CARROT & CILANTRO juice

Serves 1 • Preparation 10 minutes • Difficulty 1

2	carrots		Fresh cilantro (coriander), chopped
1	orange, peeled and seeded		Organic orange peel to garnish
1/2	lime, peeled and seeded		

1. Juice the carrots, orange, and lime into a pitcher (jug). Add the cilantro and stir well.
2. Twist the orange peel over the drink to release the fragrant oils then drop it into the drink. Serve.

FENNEL & CHERRY juice

Serves 1 • Preparation 10 minutes • Difficulty 1

3	cups (450 g) pitted cherries	1/2	bulb fennel
2	cups (300 g) seedless white grapes	1	lime, peeled and seeded

1. Juice the cherries, grapes, fennel and lime into a pitcher (jug).
2. Pour into a tall glass and serve.

APPLE & GINGER juice

Serves 1 • Preparation 10 minutes • Difficulty 1

4	organic apples, cored	1/2	teaspoon ground cinnamon
1	cup (150 g) seedless white grapes		
1	(1/2-inch/1-cm) piece ginger, peeled		

1. Juice the apples, grapes, and ginger into a pitcher (jug).
2. Stir in the cinnamon and pour into a glass.

GRAPE & CUCUMBER juice

Serves 1 • Preparation 10 minutes • Difficulty 1

1	cucumber	1	cup (50 g) fresh watercress
2	cups (300 g) seedless white grapes	1/2	lemon, peeled and seeded
2	organic apples, cored		

1. Reserve a few very thin slices of cucumber to garnish.
2. Juice the grapes, apples, cucumber, watercress, and lemon into a pitcher (jug).
3. Pour into glasses, float a slice or two of cucumber on top, and serve.

CARROT, CELERY, CUCUMBER & TOMATO *juice*

4 medium-large carrots
4 stalks celery
2 tomatoes
1 cucumber

Serves 2 • Preparation 10 minutes • Difficulty 1

1. Before you begin juicing, cut a few slices or sticks of carrot and celery to munch on with the drinks.

2. Juice the carrots, celery, tomatoes, and cucumber into a pitcher (jug). Stir the juice and pour into glasses. Serve with the carrot and cucumber.

ORANGE, CELERY & SWEET POTATO JUICE
with ginger

4   oranges, peeled and seeded
4   stalks celery
1   sweet potato
1   (1-inch/2-5-cm) piece ginger

Serves 2 • Preparation 10 minutes • Difficulty 1

1. Juice the oranges, celery, sweet potato, and ginger into a pitcher (jug).

2. Pour into glasses and serve.

Grapefruit is an excellent source of vitamin C. The red and pink varieties also contain vitamin A and carotenoids that act as strong antioxidants. A single grapefruit contains more than 150 phytonutrients that are believed to help fight against aging, allergies, heart disease, cancer, and ulcers.

GRAPEFRUIT, PEAR & SWEET POTATO juice

3	pink grapefruit, peeled and seeded
2	large organic pears, cored
1	sweet potato

Serves 1–2 • Preparation 10 minutes • Difficulty 1

1. Juice the grapefruit, pears, and sweet potato into a pitcher (jug).
2. Pour into one or two glasses and serve.

If you liked this recipe, you will love these as well.

SPICED PEAR
smoothies

**SWEET POTATO,
CARROT & APPLE** juice

**ORANGE, CELERY &
SWEET POTATO** juice

CABBAGE & APPLE JUICE with strawberries

12 stalks fresh asparagus
1/2 small green cabbage heart
2 organic apples, cored
1 medium-large carrot
6–8 fresh strawberries

Serves 2 • Preparation 10 minutes • Difficulty 1

1. Reserve two stalks of asparagus to garnish.

2. Juice the cabbage, remaining asparagus, apples, carrot, and strawberries into a pitcher (jug)

3. Pour into two glasses, garnish with the asparagus, and serve.

SPINACH, SOY & WHEAT JUICE with ginko

2 cups (100 g) fresh baby spinach leaves

3/4 cup (180 ml) soy milk

3 tablespoons chopped wheat grass

2 tablespoons pumpkin seeds

1 teaspoon ginko

Serves 1–2 • Preparation 10 minutes • Difficulty 1

1. Juice the spinach, soy milk, wheat grass, pumpkin seeds, and ginko into a pitcher (jug).

2. Pour into one or two glasses and serve.

Homemade tomato juice is preferable to most commercial brands which are often loaded with salt and preservatives. It is easy to make and will keep in the refrigerator for up to 5 days. Use more or less Tabasco sauce depending on how spicy you want the juice to be.

HOMEMADE TOMATO juice

3	pounds (1.5 kg) fresh ripe tomatoes, cored
6	stalks celery with leaves, chopped
1	medium white onion, chopped
2	tablespoons sugar
1	teaspoon salt
$^1/_2$	teaspoon freshly ground black pepper
$^1/_2$	teaspoon Tabasco sauce

Serves 12 • Preparation 15 minutes + 1 hour to cool • Cooking 30 minutes • Difficulty 1

1. Combine the tomatoes, celery, onion, sugar, salt, pepper, and Tabasco in a large saucepan over medium heat. Bring to a boil then simmer over low heat until broken down, about 30 minutes.

2. Press the mixture through a fine-mesh sieve. Let cool completely then chill in the refrigerator until needed.

If you liked this recipe, you will love these as well.

CUCUMBER & TOMATO smoothies

TOMATO smoothies

TOMATO & CELERY smoothies

PEA, MINT & CARROT juice

2   cups (300 g) fresh garden peas

4   medium carrots

$^1/_2$ cup (25 g) fresh mint leaves + extra sprigs to garnish

Serves 1 • Preparation 10 minutes • Difficulty 1

1. Juice the peas, carrots, and mint into a pitcher (jug).

2. Pour into a glass, garnish with the mint, and serve.

CITRUS & PARSLEY *juice*

3 kiwi fruits
2 oranges, peeled and seeded
1 grapefruit, peeled and seeded
$^1/_2$ cup (25 g) fresh parsley

Serves 1 • Preparation 10 minutes • Difficulty 1

1. Reserve a few cubes of kiwi to garnish. Juice the oranges, grapefruit, remaining kiwi fruit, and parsley into a pitcher (jug).

2. Pour into a glass. Push the cubes of kiwi onto a toothpick and garnish the glass before serving.

Bell peppers, also known as peppers and capsicums, are well known for their nutritional properties. They are a good source of vitamins A and C and beta-carotenes, as well as a host of other phytochemicals. Red bell peppers are more nutritious than green ones.

BELL PEPPER, CUCUMBER & CARROT juice

1	red bell pepper (capsicum), seeded and chopped
1	yellow bell pepper (capsicum), seeded and chopped
1	green bell pepper (capsicum), seeded and chopped
1	cucumber, peeled
1	carrot

Serves 2 • Preparation 10 minutes • Difficulty 1

1. Reserve a few long slices of bell pepper to serve.

2. Juice the bell peppers, cucumber, and carrot into a pitcher (jug). Pour into glasses and serve with the bell pepper.

If you liked this recipe, you will love these as well.

SPICY VEGGIE
smoothies

CARROT, SPINACH & GARLIC juice

VEGGIE & APPLE DETOX juice

Serve this pretty red drink at breakfast for a healthy start to the day.

BERRY BEST *juice*

1	cup (150 g) blueberries
1	cup (150 g) raspberries
1	cup (150 g) blackberries
1	organic apple, cored

Serves 1 • Preparation 10 minutes • Difficulty 1

1. Juice the blueberries, raspberries, blackberries, and apple into a pitcher (jug).

2. Pour into a glass and serve.

If you liked this recipe, you will love these as well.

STRAWBERRY & BLUEBERRY smoothies

FRESH RED FRUIT smoothies

BERRY BERRY smoothies

CARROT, SPINACH & GARLIC juice

3 carrots
1 cup (50 g) fresh baby spinach leaves
1 clove garlic
½ lime
Freshly ground black pepper

Serves 1 • Preparation 10 minutes • Difficulty 1

1. Juice the carrots, spinach, garlic, and lime into a pitcher (jug). Whisk in black pepper to taste.

2. Pour into a tall glass and serve.

VEGGIE & APPLE DETOX juice

4	stalks celery
2	carrots
2	organic apples, cored
1	cucumber
1	zucchini
1	red bell pepper, seeded

Serves 2–4 • Preparation 15 minutes • Difficulty 1

1. Juice the celery, carrots, apples, cucumber, zucchini, and bell pepper into a pitcher (jug).

2. Pour into glasses and serve.

You will need a juice machine or juicer for most of the recipes in this chapter. Juicers work by separating the water and nutrients from the indigestible fiber found in fruits and vegetables. You can use a blender to make them but you will get a thick, pulpy drink rather than a juice.

SPICY CARROT, APPLE & CUCUMBER juice

4	carrots
2	organic apples, cored
2	cloves garlic
1	cucumber
2	tablespoons fresh thyme + extra leaves to garnish
1	fresh red chile pepper
1	lime, peeled and seeded

Serves 2 • Preparation 10 minutes • Difficulty 1

1. Juice the carrots, apples, garlic, cucumber, thyme, chile, and lime into a pitcher (jug).

2. Pour into glasses, garnish with the extra thyme, and serve.

If you liked this recipe, you will love these as well.

SPICY VEGGIE
smoothies

CARROT, APPLE & CELERY juice

CARROT, SPINACH & GARLIC juice

ORANGE FRUIT *juice*

1   mango, pitted
1   small cantaloupe (rock) melon
2   fresh apricots, pitted
1   yellow peach, pitted
1   orange, peeled and seeded
1   grapefruit, peeled and seeded

Serves 2 • Preparation 10 minutes • Difficulty 1

1. Juice the mango, melon, apricots, peach, orange, and grapefruit into a pitcher (jug).

2. Pour into glasses and serve.

EXOTIC FRUIT cream

1   small sweet pineapple
1   mango, pitted
3   passion fruits
1   cup (250 ml) plain yogurt

Serves 2 • Preparation 10 minutes • Difficulty 1

1. Reserve a tablespoon of passion fruit pulp to garnish.

2. Juice the pineapple, mango, and passion fruit into a pitcher (jug). Stir in the yogurt.

3. Pour into glasses, garnish with the reserved passion fruit pulp, and serve.

INDEX